Introduction

Hi, I am Chris and I am a 'Charlie'. This is how Cypriots refer to people born in the UK of Cypriot parents, as I was. I think we get this name from something to do with Prince Charles, as HIS father is Greek. I lived most of my life in the UK, 53 years, and then moved to Cyprus where I have been living for coming up to 11 years. Although I lived in the UK with my three siblings, my parents brought us up in a traditional and customary Cypriot way. I had visited Cyprus many times and gained knowledge of both worlds. Don't get me wrong, I love the UK, it gave me the opportunity to be where I am, but I equally love Cyprus. They both have their merits, but also both have their downfalls, and in MY opinion for what it's worth, you couldn't get two peoples more different.

What follows is my humorous take on life in Cyprus. It is written very much tongue in cheek and is not meant to insult or offend. What I am trying to portray in this book are the actions and reactions to certain situations and events by the Cypriot. Compare them to your average English person and see the difference.

Once you have mastered the Cypriots idiosyncrasies, you can live very happily by their side....maybe. So pour yourself Ouzo or a Cypriot coffee, put your feet up and enjoy.

1.
The Doctors Surgery.

Here in Cyprus the only actual Doctors surgeries are the private ones which cost a fortune just to walk through the door, unlike the UK where there will be an NHS group practice near you. The majority of us Cypriots use the state Hospitals. This is where you come to see a GP or a Specialist, Cardiologist, Urologist etc. These Doctors are paid by the state for us that are in a state.

Going to the Hospital is a long drawn out agonizing affair. Expect to lose half a day of your life going to see a Doctor about your terrible dose of Flu, Cypriots do tend to visit the Doc' at the drop of a hat. They are Hypochondriacs, well, they did invent the word! You have arrived at the Hospital where you will spend at least half an hour trying to park. You will see cars parked in ways you have never seen before! When a Cypriot goes anywhere, he/she feels the need to actually park their car INSIDE the shop/Hospital, or wherever they are going. If they can't, they feel cheated, so they will park stupidly, illegally, to be as near the entrance as possible.

2.

This is why a certain fast food place that begins with 'McD' does so well over here; you don't even have to get out the car at the drive through!

Once you realize that the phrase, 'if you can't beat them join them' also applies to you and you abandon your car up the kerb and on a corner, a helpful Cypriot watching you from afar will shout......

"RE BELLO ENGLESO, YOU CUNT PUKING THERE!"

Now call me pedantic, but I look every bit a Cypriot, dark skin, hairy with a bolshie walk, so what gives me away as a 'BELLO ENGLESO' (Stupid English), I don't know! Anyway I digress...

You carry on walking, pretending you ARE an Engleso, and head for the Hospital entrance. You arrive at the out patients entrance where you are met by half a dozen men, all with a cigarette in their mouth, coughing and spluttering and trying to talk at the same time. They are telling each other how long they have had this lingering cough, and that their Doctor knows shit all about coughs!!

One said, "I only smoking this soft one's", by that he meant low tar cigarettes, the fact he smoked three packs a day was irrelevant!

After you have gone through the 'interrogation', i.e. 'who's son are you?' 'What village are you from?' 'How much did your house cost?' These are standard questions asked when meeting new people for the first time; you enter the Hospital to go to reception. The Hospital administration in their wisdom, have located the receptionists right in front of the entrance door! There is a row of receptionists behind a high security glass window with little slots in the bottom so you can talk to them. It looks more like a Bank.

It looks and feels like the whole of Larnaca has decided to be ill on the same day you have had to pay a visit. I have never seen so much chaos anywhere! Even Cattle are more organized. There is a row of six receptionists, and the queues, if you can call them that are just a mass of moving bodies. Recently someone had this epiphany that if they put up a ribbon barrier, much like at the Airport, it would be a little more civilized, and it is to a point, but you still get the occasional old Yiayia or Bappou, (Grandma or Grandpa), who announces to everyone in a pitiful voice how ill they are and should be allowed to jump the queue! Sometimes they don't even do that, suddenly, their chronic back pain goes away long enough for them to bend right down and duck under the barrier to the front of the queue! Who is going to confront an old man or woman with a walking stick?

So, why are we queuing? Well, you have to register the fact that you are in the Hospital. You pay your three Euros for a GP or six Euros for a specialist. Your prescription book is stamped and you are allocated a Doctor if you don't request a particular Doctor.

4.

You are then sent on your way to the room your Doctor is holding his surgery to queue…again! You have now been away from home for well over an hour and you haven't seen a Doctor yet!

You now find yourself in a huge expanse of space with doors on either side. Each door is numbered and the occupying Doctors name is also displayed. We have about twenty doors! You look for your number, bearing in mind that the numbers don't necessarily run in sequence, and you find your Doctor. Outside his door you will find about ten chairs for the thirty patients?? The Yiayias and Bappous have already claimed them, and there they will stay rigidly until they are called or the Turks invade again. If you are lucky enough, or perhaps I should say Unlucky enough, to have an appointment, expect to still be waiting at least for an hour after the actual time you were given. This is called 'Cyprus time'.

This area of the Hospital has been witness to many a heated argument. This helps the time go by, and a great source of amusement, for me anyway whilst I wait. I must explain that these days the only reason I go to the Hospital is for my repeat prescription for my Heart condition, which I may add is under control. So picture this; you have tenish chairs occupied by mostly the older ones, and you have about fifteen people leaning against the pillars that hold the Hospital up, and in various positions around the walls. There is a heavily pregnant women with two brats, oops sorry, children running about shouting and screaming and generally making a nuisance of themselves. The mother is too tired and drained to try and stop them, and nobody is going to give their chair up. Eventually, the Doctor sticks her head out of the door and asks for the mother to control and keep her kids quiet and slams the door shut.

This results in everyone glaring at the mother and tutting at her. I then dared to speak. I dared suggest that although it wasn't the pregnant lady with the kids turn, to let her go next, thus taking the strain off her and giving our ears a break. The reaction I got was worse than if I had just announced that their pensions would cease as from now!!

"MA BELANES? ESHI BOU TES EXI BOU IME THAME!!"
("Have you gone mad, I have been here since 6am"?)

Irrelevant that Hospital reception doesn't open until 7.30am. Somebody else said….

"AFISTI NA BAI BROTI NA ISIXASOME"
("Let her go first so we can get some peace")

A back and forth argument between the two patients continued, both standing up now and pointing fingers and voices getting louder and getting close to blows. I watched in awe. The really funny bit though is while everybody was distracted taking bets on who would win this private civil war, the Doctor had opened the door and quietly called the lady in unbeknown to anyone. She obviously agreed with my thoughts.

I now turned my attention to two old ladies clad in Black who were sitting near me. I decided to eavesdrop, not that I needed to as everyone could hear them anyway. Cypriots tend to shout a lot, they think the louder they talk that the point they are making is a correct one. Most Cypriots think that they know best, whatever you have he has more. This is the conversation the old ladies had; in Cypriot but for obvious reasons I will write in English, and this actually happened.

6.

First lady: "Hi, are you from Larnaca?"

Second lady: "No, I'm from Troulli"

First: "So what's wrong with you then?"

Second: "Oh, I have a bad pain in my knee"

First: "Oh really, so do I"

Second: "Mine really hurts"

First: "So does mine, it's as if someone is stabbing it"

Second: "Mine too, but not with a knife, with a SWORD!"

First: "No, no mine is more like an AXE!"

Then there is a pause. I'm trying not to laugh out loud.

First: "Are you taking anything for it?"

Second: "Yes, Doctor gave me some anti inflammatory pills, but it still hurts"

First: "Yes, MY pills are the size of Horse pills!"

Second: "Mine are SO big, I have to cut them in half so I can swallow them!"

Another pause…

First: "Can you walk on it ok?"

Second: "Not really it's too pain full"

First: "I can't walk on mine"

Second: "How did you get here then?"

First: "Well I didn't walk! My son helped me"

Second: "My son was far too busy with his business"

First: "MY son has a business"

Second: "Well mine is a Plumber"

First: "Mine is an Electrician, he USED to be a Plumber but Electricians earn more"

Second: "Says who?"

First: "My son does and he should know, he has done both!"

Second: "Maybe he was a rubbish Plumber?"

First: "He was the best in the village!"

Second: "Yes, says you"

First: "Are you calling me a liar?"

Can you see where this is going? We started politely talking about our ailments, and we are now headed for another civil war!

After what felt like an eternity, it was my turn. I went into the room and put my prescription book on the desk and inform the Doctor that it's just a repeat prescription. She flicked through the book to find the previous one to copy. She hesitated and said,
 "I can't give you this medication your Cardiologist has to prescribe it"
I explain that he DID prescribe it; it's just a repeat prescription. I have this palaver every six months! I explain that I see my Cardiologist every six months but he is only allowed to give me three months of medication. He told me the other three months would be given to me by any other GP. She mumbled under her breath and wrote out the prescription. What should have taken three minutes had taken ten! And it doesn't end there, oh no, now you have to go to the Hospital Pharmacy to QUEUE up for your medication.

You walk across the Hospital grounds to the furthest point away from the Doctors surgeries and enter the building again, and lo and behold, a massive queue of all the people you saw when you very first came in and registered! There are three dispensing windows but only two are ever open no matter how busy it is! Another half an hour of pushing and elbowing and arguing....

All I can say is 'Don't be ill in Cyprus!' or go private if you can afford it.

9.

The Church

Please allow me to state that I am not a particularly religious person. I do believe in an ultimate power, but that's another book. In Cyprus you HAVE to be religious even if you are not, if you know what I mean. Basically you don't shout it from the roof tops that you don't believe in God. I go to church when I HAVE to, weddings, funerals, and christenings and occasionally at Easter time as it's such an event here in Cyprus, more so than Christmas.

We arrive at the Church for a wedding ceremony. On arrival the parking situation is much like the Hospital car park, everybody as close to the Church entrance as possible. If you were unlucky enough to arrive FIRST, you will definitely be leaving LAST, simply because you have been hemmed in on all sides! You would be hard pushed to get a cigarette paper between your car and any other. I always park in what is theoretically an empty car park because everybody is parked in the Church vestibule!

As you approach the Church entrance you can see scattered around the walls of the Church, groups of people that keep the tobacco companies in business, puffing away and talking about last night's football match, or Politics or Religion, the three things my Dad always told me NOT to discuss with Cypriots…Why? Because whatever your view on the mentioned subjects, you will be shouted down! You cannot possibly know more than a Cypriot on these subjects. If you insist, the voice gets louder; the finger starts waving and sometimes even jabbing!

There are certain unspoken rules when in such a Holy place, 'Quiet', 'Be humble', Don't turn your back on the Altar unless you are leaving', 'Dress respectably', 'Never swear inside a Church', 'No smoking', shall I go on? Well, you can throw all of that out of the window! Apart from a minority who do abide by these rules, everybody else sees it as a reason for a get together and to spread the latest gossip.

The joining of the couple is in full swing, but you wouldn't know it judging by the actions of the throng of people in the Church. There were kids screaming and running up and down the aisles, and there were a hundred different conversations going on, none of which had anything to do with the actual event we were there for.

I listened in on a conversation between two Black clad Yiayias who looked like 'Ninjas'.

Just to enlighten you, the 'Black clad Ninjas' are this way because they are widows. They dress like this as a sign of respect for their dear departed. My Yiayia, (above), was a widow at 30 something, and was in Black until she died at the age of 98, God rest her soul. There are a LOT of Black clad ladies in Cyprus. Anyway, Black is Black, so why was one old lady telling the other why HER Black Cardigan was better than her friends Black Cardigan? They are BOTH Black!! No, her one was better because her daughter had brought it back from 'ANGLIA' so it HAD to be better!

"AGORASEN TO BOU TO NTEBENHUMS"
(She bought it in Debenhams).

Truth be known, both Cardigans were probably made in the same factory in India!

I turned my attention to the two gentlemen in front of me. I use the term 'gentlemen' very loosely. One kept looking to his left to the row of pews adjacent to ours. Eventually he nudged the man standing at his side and whispered in his ear…

"GITA TIN JINI!" (Take a look at her!)

The man turns and has a look…

"AMAN INTA GOLOS" (Wow what an arse!)

So now we are blaspheming, but then, as if by some miracle, a pang of conscience strikes them…

"EN FOUSTA TOUTI NA FORESI STO SBITI TOU THEOU!"
(Is that a skirt to wear in the house of God?)

"THEN ANTREBETE GATHOLOU!"
(She has no shame!)

So the original lecherous remarks are forgiven by God himself. The couple is now married, but nobody is aware apart from the closest relatives. They all stampede out of the Church at the same time, and on to their awaiting cars. Ninety percent of them can't even get INTO their cars as they are so closely parked together, and here ensues another civil war!

Like I said, I don't go to Church much!!

14.

The Supermarket.

Supermarket shopping, I will shamelessly admit, I do not do if I can help it. This is one of those rare occasions when I have accompanied my wife. So you park sensibly…..

Well why only use one space when you can use two!?

We grab a trolley and enter the store. We are immediately accosted by two lovely ladies informing us that '7UP' is on special offer today and that we should buy a couple of cases. My wife and daughter, being seasoned shoppers, kept on walking, I have stopped to listen to their logical marketing speech, nothing to do with the fact that one of them was a 'DD' in hat size!

"Are you coming or what? You don't even like '7UP'!" shouts my wife. I shrug at the girls and catch her up. My wife knows exactly where she is going and my daughter is at her side and I follow behind like a lost Lamb.

My wife gives instructions to my daughter to go and get certain items and bring them back to save time. She is also an experienced shopper. We are quite organized but the rest of the store most certainly is not! We have to be the most disorganized nation in the World…bless us.

The reason I am here at all is to give my wife some moral support, you see, she is English, and she wants to have a go at ordering some Mince at the meat counter but in Cypriot…Go girl!

"ENA KILO GAEMA VOTHINO SE BARAKALO"
(A kilo of Beef mince if you please.)

We have practiced this at home, in the car on the way to the store, walking around the store, and I must say she had it down perfect, I was very proud of her. At the fresh meat counter there is a 'ticket' system, take a ticket and wait for your number to be called…yeah, yeah! This is CYPRUS! There is a mass of bodies three deep in front of the counter, all in hurry and only half with a ticket. A woman suddenly shouts from the back and over the crowd…

"YIASOU NICO MOU, THOS MOU LIGO SOUVLAKI GE VIASOME"
(Hello my Nic, give me some souvlaki, (pork pieces), I'm in a hurry)

Apparently in Cyprus, the old adage 'It's not what you know but who you know' stands and she obviously knew Nico! Worse still, instead of telling her to wait her turn, he serves her first!

Somebody else shouts out…

"EN KAFKA SOU RE NICO?"
(Is she your mistress Nico?)

You have to laugh or go insane. Everybody lets this one go,
but then it happened again. A shout from the back…

"RE GIORGO ENA KOTOBOULO RE"
(Oi! George, (the other butcher), a chicken)

That was it, the signal for yet another civil war! I heard the
butchers called things I had never heard before, and just as
bad coming back at them, and I promise they were not words
of endearment.

I stand patiently with my wife who is quietly reciting the
words over and over to herself. I tell her how well she is doing
and that it sounds perfect. Eventually, Nico looks at my wife
and says…

"NE?" (Yes?)

My wife answers nice and clearly and perfectly…

"ENA KILO GAEMA VOTHINO SE BARAKALO"

Nico just stood staring at her with a puzzled look on his face
and then says…

"Why you no tokking in englesiga?"

I give up!!

We walk up an aisle to the Fruit and Vegetables where everyone is squeezing the life out of Oranges, Pears etc to see if they are ripe. The trouble is, they ARE ripe and they just end up with a handful of mush which they put back on the shelf!

Up the next aisle where there is a 'barricade' half way up. Two women with their trolleys right across the aisle, discussing what they are going to cook tonight and without a care in the world that we were coming through, we were invisible. Another civil war was avoided when my Nine year old daughter, in a very loud voice and in Cypriot said…

"THA BERASOME!"
(We WILL pass!)

Nobody confronts a child here!

We are nearly done. We get in the queue at the checkout, Lol! QUEUE? There is no such thing in Cyprus as you may have gathered, but we attempt to be orderly. The girl at the till looks like she is about to burst into tears, obviously not happy in her job. We load our shopping neatly onto the conveyor belt. The girl picks up our first item and is about to 'beep' it with her magic gun, when an old man physically shoves my wife out the way, and waves a loaf of bread in the girls face, and says…

"TOUTO EXO HATE!"
(I have this, hurry!)

I didn't know who to reprimand first, the ill mannered obnoxious old man, or the girl for taking his loaf and 'beeping' it!! There is a check out desk for ten items or less a couple of tills away!

When the girl stopped glaring at us as if WE had done something wrong, she started 'beeping' our stuff. My daughter and I go to the other end of the chute to start packing our goods into the bags. She beeped the Baked Beans and literally threw them down the chute towards us, then she threw the Tuna, beeped the bread threw it picked up MY Chocolate Digestives and THREW them!! That was it! That broke the Camel's back! I picked up the Digestives and threw them straight back and said, in Cypriot...

"If I wanted broken biscuits, I would have paid less and bought broken biscuits!"

Then my wife joined in telling her that they are OUR goods and to refrain from throwing them about. The girl looked at us both, for a bit, then had the cheek to say....

"The goods are NOT yours officially as they have not been paid for yet!"

Whatever happened to courtesy to the customer? My wife is not to be messed with; she did nothing more then tell the girl that as the goods were still HERS, she wouldn't mind putting them all back!!

We headed out the store empty handed.

19.

Clothes shopping

It's Saturday morning and I am off out to buy a pair of Sandals.
"Where are you going?" asked my wife.

"Off to buy a pair of sandals" I replied.

"Oh, hang on, we will come with you, I need to find a Navy Blue skirt for work" she added.

Just what I wanted…NOT! Don't get me wrong, I love the company of my family, but when a bloke goes shopping for something, he knows what he wants, in this case a pair of sandals. I will go into the nearest shoe shop, find the sandals that I like, pay for them and leave, job done! Shopping with one and a half women doesn't work that way, and it didn't….

I did my 'parking' and we went into the shoe shop.

Well at least he was considerate enough not to park in the disabled bay!

Anyway, once in the shop I found a pair of sandals I liked within five minutes and we went to the cash out desk. Behind the counter sat a lady who was dressed as if she was going to a night club, or she had been to a night club and had come straight to work. She had a mobile phone stuck to her ear and was talking about a film she had watched to whoever was at the other end. We stood patiently at the desk waiting for her to finish. She had seen us but obviously her conversation was far more important, where do they get these people? After a while when it became apparent to me that she was in no hurry, I started to tap the sandals on the desk, and what was her reaction? Instead of doing the right thing by doing her job and serving us, she tutted and moved further down the counter so she could carry on her conversation! They say that there is a financial crisis here in Cyprus, but obviously this shop was not affected!

"Do you WANT paying for these or shall I just take them?" I asked.

She STILL didn't end her conversation, she said into the phone...

"ENA LEPTO EXO BELATI"
(Wait a minute I have a customer)

She checked me out, but continued her conversation as she did so!

We are out of there, next stop find a skirt. We go into the first shop yes I said first shop because you know it's not going to end there! It's obligatory to enter at the very minimum four shops before returning to the first shop to buy your whatever. So, we are back in the first shop and my wife asks for the two skirts she saw earlier so she can try them on....again. It's Saturday afternoon and it's quite busy. The two changing rooms are both occupied, so we sit on the chairs provided to wait our turn. On this occasion the staff were great, it's the customers that were my source of amusement.

A couple of facts, the 'average' ladies size in the UK are a size 12, in Cyprus it's a 14 and Pear shaped. The Cypriot girl/woman will insist she is a size 8 or 10 and will ONLY buy an 8 or 10. She will live on Lettuce leaves for a month before going shopping for clothes. A lot of the cleverer shops don't have 8-10-12-14; they have Small, Medium or Large. The girls here are avid followers of fashion, but nobody has told them that today's fashion was fashionable in the 90's in the rest of the world.

We are watching Sophie and her friend Maro shopping for a Purple pair of leggings...yes Purple.

"NA TA THOGIMASO"
(I'll try them on) says Sophie.

She disappeared into the changing room and eventually reappeared. I wished she hadn't! I don't know if her friend Maro was being polite and didn't want to hurt her friend's feelings, but she squealed…

"O SOPHIA MOU, INE IBEROXA BANO SOU!"
(Oh my Sophia they look fantastic on you).

I looked at my wife, and then I had to have another look at Sophie. Sophie wasn't what I would call a slim girl, and I have my reservations as to who can wear leggings and who shouldn't, and I'm sorry, but Sophie certainly shouldn't! She not only had a spare tyre for a tractor wheel, but she had enough spare tyres for a 14 wheeler flat bed container lorry! It looked hideous. Maro thought they looked great so she bought them?

23.

In the work place.

Getting back to the saying, 'It's not what you know it's who you know'…nepotism is rife in Cyprus, more so now in this time of crisis. If you are not very close to someone, who knows someone, you haven't got too much hope of a job.

My wife is lucky enough to have a job, but she got that because my mum's cousin comes from the same village as Mixalis, who is very close to Mr.? Who owns a string of supermarkets amongst other things, who is also from the same village as mum! Get it? He hadn't even met my wife, but she got the job in accounts on the strength of all that.

Let's take the 'office' working environment. In my experience, and what is logical, an environment in ANY working arena is where the employees work closely together, unselfishly, and as a team, 'Team work'. This ensures a smooth flow of whatever needs to be done with the minimum of effort. Unfortunately in Cyprus this rule does not apply!

Imagine an office space with four desks and an employee sat at each one. Each employee has their job/duty to perform. Would you be surprised to know that neither one knows the others job? This is not because they are stupid, it's because each one 'GUARDS' their job like one would the President on a visit to another nation! Each employee acts like an MI5 agent! Secretive, guarded, etc. and why? A few reasons; It's all to do with holding on to their jobs. The more the others know about their particular job, the more dispensable it makes them; they see it as a threat. Another reason would be that someone might point out that what they are doing is wrong and there is an easier way to do it this cannot be allowed because nobody knows better than them, they know best...always! If anyone is absent for any length of time, their work will be stacked up on their desk for when they get back, this of course halts all progress in the office as nobody dares approach the absent persons work. When they return to work, that person then takes great joy in telling everyone how indispensable they must be as nobody knew how to do their work!?

Nobody dares ask for assistance as this is a great sign of weakness and terrible inefficiency. To admit you are not coping is like admitting you are of a lower standard then your colleagues, so you carry on cocking it up until someone spots your errors, THEN you can blame it on somebody else!

The Untouchables

Red tape, officialdom and bureaucracy in bucketfuls. If you have the misfortune to deal with any government office, which you will one way or the other, these are things to expect. The people that are employed in a government run office are a 'special and unique' breed. They truly believe that because they are employed by the government, puts them way above everybody else…no exceptions! The rest of us are mere minions scratching out a living and who couldn't even do that without THEIR help. They believe they have a job for life, because to get a government job, your Dad IS the President OR his brother! 'The Untouchables'.

When you first get off the Plane to start your new life in Cyprus, nobody greets you with a 'Do's Don'ts and How to' in Cyprus book. Maybe they should? (Maybe this one?). I will give you here just ONE of my experiences/escapades with my brush with the 'Untouchables'.

A relative of mine thought that it would be wise to apply for
'Cypriot Citizenship' as this would open many doors for me,
and at the very least make my journey into Cyprus life
smoother. I was eligible to make this application as both my
parents are Cypriot.

First stop is go to the Larnaca Town Hall and get an
application form, relatively easy, I did have my first taste of
queuing here, but it was a novelty then. I took the two page
application form home to get assistance in filling it out. My
Greek reading and writing are limited, and as the forms only
came in Greek then…the first stumbling block! With the form
filled, I returned to the Town hall. I queued for half an hour
and eventually got to see someone. They informed me that the
person who deals with these applications is only available
Mondays and Fridays, today is Tuesday!! Why didn't they tell
me this when I picked up the forms? Never mind, I forgive
them and return on the Friday. This time I queue for an hour!
To see the lady who deals with this. She greets me politely
enough and I hand over my completed forms, which she
flicked through.

"Can I see your Passport, Birth Certificate, your daughter's
Birth Certificate, and your Marriage Certificate…please?"

"What? Nobody told me to bring all that!"

"Sorry, (Cypriot shrug of shoulders), can't proceed with the
application without these documents"

I am getting a little angry now. This is my third visit to the Town Hall and I have got nowhere. I returned on Monday with the required documentation, and I queue for another hour. The lady smiles broadly at me as if mocking me, but she is polite. I put the application forms with the documents on the desk in front of her. She looks through again, nodding approvingly as she does so. She then pushes everything away from her and towards me and says…

"Very good, but we need the originals"

I look at her in stunned silence…

"You didn't SAY that, I assumed copies would be fine"

"(Cyprus shrug), well they are not! Originals please".

I grabbed everything off the desk and left mumbling to myself as I go. So, I wait until Friday and return with the 'originals' of the documents. This time I queue for one and a half hours! It is steaming hot, and I am already irritable. I gently put everything onto the desk.

"Bravo Christakis" she said condescendingly. She satisfies herself that everything is in order and starts stamping things. YEAH! Nearly out of here…NOT"

"I can't seem to find your parents Marriage Certificate"

I don't believe it!!!!

"When did you say you wanted that?"

"Well it's obvious we want that, otherwise how do we know they are your parents?"

"Well does it matter? It's me who is applying for citizenship".

"(Cyprus shrug), Sorry but we need to see it"

F**K ME! This is ridiculous. Where am I supposed to get my parents marriage certificate? My Dad is deceased, my Mum is 84 years old and is in the UK, and she probably threw it away when they got divorced! I got home and phoned my Mum. Yep, she threw it away when they got divorced!

I had to write to a place in Scotland to get a copy. It cost me £50. It was a month later before I returned to the Town Hall for the 5th time! After yet another forty five minutes of queuing, I get to see Miss helpful.

"Great, great now we can finish up"

"Thank God for that"

She stamped some more, put everything in a nice little folder and handed it to me.

"All done, welcome to Cyprus Christakis" she said shaking my hand.

"Just take the folder with the passport photo to the front desk and they will make up your ID card"

"WHAT FU**KING PASSPORT PHOTO?"

I couldn't believe my ears, I was fuming, my neck and ears felt really hot and I exploded! I threw the whole file at her and yelled that I would rather remain English if this is the way you treat your own, and I turned to leave.

She somehow managed to get me to sit down and pacify me. She gave me back the file and told me ONE more visit and it would all be over. I calmed down. I DID go back with a photo and I was in and out in half an hour.

So it took SIX visits simply because absolutely no information was forthcoming or volunteered, you have to find out the hard way.

They could have had, WITH the application forms, a list of what to produce when making your application....

How hard would that have been?

The Beach

There is a beach to suit everyone's taste here in Cyprus. There is a beach called 'Mackenzie' beach, it is lined with trendy bars and restaurants used mainly by the…well the 'trendiest' it's not unusual to see the likes of Peter Andre milling about here.

There is a promenade/beach called 'Finigouthes' which is more geared up for the tourist. Here you will find 'McDonalds', 'Kentucky', 'Pizza Hut' etc. because apparently some tourists don't like 'Foreign muck' to quote an English friend of mine…why come to a foreign country then?

There are beautiful unspoilt hidden coves which you will have to hunt for.

There are beaches between the Hotels that line Dhekalia road seafront which the Hotels haven't claimed…yet!

There is even a nudist beach, but I don't know where that is!

It's easy to spot the tourist, apart from the Union Jack shorts, the knotted handkerchief on the head, a can or bottle of beer in hand, and that is just the women! They are usually burnt to a crisp within two hours of landing on Cypriot soil no matter what factor lotion they have smeared on.

All that said it's even EASIER to spot the Cypriot! And as it's a book about Cypriots in Cyprus, I'll talk about them.

There are many kinds of Cypriot beach frequenters, (is that a word? Well it is now), but I will concentrate on the four main ones.

First let's take the 'LONE SUNBATHER', usually a female. She has absolutely no intention of getting wet. She has an immaculate hair do or a hat that wouldn't look out of place at Ascot. Her sunglasses are 'Gucci', and her bikini looks like it would disintegrate if she DID get in the water! She is a professional Sun worshipper.

She gently toasts herself evenly making sure to turn every five minutes and refreshing her lotion each time. She will stand up now and then to brush off the four grains of sand the breeze may have blown onto her towel and another three grains off her body, flicking at them as they were something nasty a dog had left behind…oh, and so we can get another look at her perfect body.

Moving on to the 'TWO GIRLS TOGETHER' situation. These two are the exact opposite of our first lady. Not only have they every intention of getting soaked, they have brought with them a pump action water pistol each to spray each other and anybody else in the vicinity. Later, the Frisbee comes out and goes everywhere but to each other. Then the bats and ball comes out…there is something naughty about watching two girls playing bat and ball?

A little way up the beach is the 'TWO BOYS TOGETHER' who have slowly, inch by inch, got closer as if on 'Magic towels' as opposed to Magic Carpets. This is when the game of...well, the game of the Birds and Bees starts! We now have to get each other's attention so the water pistols come out again and OOPS! They 'accidently' wet the boys. After numerous warnings from the boys that if it should happen again the girls would get a dunking in the sea, they accidently get squirted again...and there you have it, 'Physical contact' as both girls get a ducking, giggling like, like, well like two girls...the Birds and Bees!

Fanfare of trumpets Here they come! You can hear them from the car park! That special breed of beach invader, 'THE CYPRIOT FAMILY' Yiayia and all. First to land on the beach is Dad, he has come to survey the beach and stake a claim. He thunders on to the beach like a Sumo wrestler all nineteen stone of him! I'm sure he hasn't seen his Willy for years. Nobody has dared tell him he looks ridiculous in 'Speedos' if you can find them that is. He is as bald as a baby's bum, but his body hasn't been so lucky, you can just make out patches of skin between the masses of hair, he would give a Silver Back Gorilla a run for his money.

He is followed by his three 'mini-me's', not quite the same weight, but catching up quickly. Two boys, probably ten months between them so they look like twins, and a daughter a bit older who will probably have to start shaving soon.

And here comes the wife, and such a contrast you have never seen! The lady is positively anorexic! A stick insect has more meat on it! It leaves you wondering how on earth they had children together; surely any sexual encounter between them would result in her being severely injured? She has her arm through Yiayias arm that can hardly walk on a hard surface never mind sand! Why are they torturing her so? I can only assume it's to look after the 'Weebles'.

They stake their claim by sticking a pole in the sand with an umbrella. The Dad, as if marking his territory, walks backwards dragging his heel in the sand around the pole, he claims about an Acre! This is why…

He returns to the pickup truck with the eldest weeble and comes back with three sun loungers and another umbrella. Second trip he comes back with a plastic table and four chairs. The third trip he returns with a Gazebo! Which they erect in record time as they have done it so many times. Fourth trip is the BBQ, coal and firelighters. Fifth trip are the cold boxes, one with the meat in it, one with salads and fruit, and one with the beers and other cold drinks. The piste de resistance, on the sixth trip, an amplifier, two speakers and a CD player and a small generator that will also power the two halogen lamps that come on the seventh trip! I think they are here for the long term!

34.

Social gatherings.

Weddings, Christenings, in fact any mass gathering of people.
Basically, these gatherings are a great place for the men to
show off their new car, new suit, new haircut or new trendy
jeans. Also a competition who can smoke the most, drink the
most, and it always culminates into a dancing competition…'a
dance off'.

For the women it's who can wear the most outrageous dress,
or shortest skirt, or highest heels and Reddest lipstick.

For kids it's just a massive play area where they can run
amuck and get sick because they have drunk too much coke
and ate too much cake.

Standard procedure at functions is that the men all eventually
end up sitting together away from their women folk. I don't
know why this is, I would much rather sit with a bunch of
women! Must be a chauvinist thing. The men sit around
discussing football, politics and religion and the women
discuss their men!

At one such function, I had cause to be more embarrassed
then I had ever been before…

Sitting at our table was a young Black couple from Jamaica.
They had by their side in a pram a new born baby. A Yiayia
walking past decided to stop and admire it. She bent down to
the pram and started making all the usual noises, goo-goo
gaga, and said out loud in her pigeon English…

"Ooo, isen she omorfi (pretty)" and as she stood to walk away, she mumbled under her breath...

"MAVRO SHILA!" (Black bitch!)

The couple looked at her with broad grins and said in PERFECT GREEK,

"Thank you and it's a boy" They got up and left.

Lesson here; don't judge a book by its cover!

Too much too soon.

I would like to share my opinion on why I think Cypriots are the way they are. I have thought it over and it makes perfect sense to me.

Let's go back about fifty years. Cypriots have always been a simple people, and by that I don't mean stupid... necessarily! They had a simple life style. Simple, casual living laid back attitude, their favorite saying, which is applied to most things, is 'Siga, siga' (slowly, slowly). Why do today that which you can just as easily do tomorrow? Get the idea?

You still had the rich and poor but the divide wasn't as wide. The rich were considered to be the educated ones, Doctor, Lawyers, Teachers etc. and the poor were the Farmers, field workers and Shepherds. Then less than fifty years ago something absolutely amazing happened that would turn everything on its head, the poorest became the richest overnight! How?
The Sheep and Goat herders who reared their animals to milk and make 'Halloumi' cheese to sell, also the Milk was sold and of course their meat was also great on the BBQ. These people had a Donkey for transport, (those were the days), and they had a home built of mud and hay with no windows or doors which was sitting on acres of land that was at the time worthless. These are the people I meant were a simple people, a naïve people, but very happy people.

 They worked hard to send their sons and daughters abroad for a better education, America, Greece the UK. Then it happened…'Property Developers' a hungry new breed with money! They came from all over. They would approach a poor Mr. Pappadoulou who had ten acres of land that was only good for grazing his thirty Sheep and Goats, and they gave him… a Million pounds!! Mr. Stavros Pappadoulou, whose highlight in life was when he opened his handkerchief to see what his wife had given him for lunch, now had a Million pounds! Stavros, who lost fifty cents at the Cafene yesterday playing Tavli, (Backgammon), and was still worrying about it today, now, has a Million pounds!

The Developer has built Stavros a four bed roomed Villa with pool as part of the agreement, so he has gone from a one roomed mud hut to a Villa. The Donkey has gone, and despite not having a driving lesson in his life, he now owns a brand new Mercedes, and so do his two sons and daughter.

From this:

To this:

I guess the point I'm trying to make is that generally, the Cypriot doesn't know how to cope with his new found wealth and modernization simply because he has never had it!

The Cinema

What an experience going to the Cinema in Cyprus is! It's amazing!

In the UK, we go to the Cinema and sit with our wife, girlfriend or friend and watch a film. There is occasional laughter if it's a comedy, but other than that, the old 'British' reserve kicks in and we watch in silence. It's a private experience, not so in Cyprus…

In Cyprus it's like the audience is actually IN the film! They are the actors. It's like 'Saturday morning pictures' but for adults. After loading up with a bucket of popcorn, packets of M&M's, a gallon cup of Coke, they sit in anticipation waiting for the lights to go down. The lights eventually go down and all the conversations and mumbling stops. The film starts, 'Twilight Saga', and so do the audience with a vengeance! They start screaming and booing at the bad guys, yelling, clapping and whistling at the good guys, laughter wherever necessary, I have never seen an audience so involved and elated. I loved it!!

The film was crap, but watching the people was Oscar worthy!

Driving

OMG! I don't know where to start. It's almost like they have read the 'Highway Code', (I think we have one?), then they do the exact opposite! Each and every driver believes that they actually do OWN the roads, and all the other drivers are trespassing on them!

They will insist that traffic lights are for tourists only. Zebra crossings are a parking bay, or decoration for the boring Black tarmac. They think a 'NO ENTRY' sign is a Burger King sign, and a 'ONE WAY STREET' sign is showing them which direction the wind is blowing.

The car itself, whether it is a top of the range Mercedes or a clapped out Skoda, only has ONE light setting, 'FULL BEAM'! The rear view mirror and side mirrors are for applying your makeup or shaving! The car horn is for saying Hello, Goodbye or just to annoy the trespassing person in front. The indicators…well what indicators? The radio is on just to entertain pedestrians, or people who like music at 2am whilst they sleep, and the aerial is for putting your favorite football team's flag on. The seat belts are for strapping your latest purchase from IKEA onto the seat, or the water bottle for your cooler, or your shopping even, but NOT for your 4/5 year old child who is standing on the front seat with its hands on the dashboard to steady his/herself. I even saw a mother with a child on her lap as she drove! I have seen a bloke steering with his knees on a motorway, with a mobile phone in one hand and a can of fizzy in the other! Mobile phones are a must have accessory whilst driving. Cyclists and motorcyclists are completely invisible, even when going up the motorway the wrong way!

NO...NO...NO!

YESSS...YES HANDS FREE!

Food

The Cypriots most important pastime, food, second only to their mobile phones. A Cypriot wife has her work cut out as far as cooking is concerned, because no matter how good her cooking is, it will never be better than her Mother in laws!

Somebody, not too far from this keyboard used to say, "Not as good as my mum's" more than he should. One day, my wife, oops I mean HIS wife, served him some meat balls and they were the best he had ever tasted, and he told his wife so.

"What better than your mums?" she asked.

"Yes they were excellent".

This pleased her so much that she did nothing more than invites her in laws to dinner for the next day. She was going to make some…meat balls.

The wife brought the meat balls to the table and said with pride, "Chris, (oops again), Spyros said my meat balls are better than yours mum" Mum scowled at Spyros. After tasting them she said condescendingly, "They were delicious darling, very nice indeed." When the wife was clearing the table and out of ear shot, Spyros mum leant over and whispered in his ear, "THELOUN ALAS!" (They need more salt!). Competitive or what?

It's coming up to Easter and most of the population of Cyprus is going on a 40 day fasting period. No Oils, no dairy produce and worst of all no MEAT!

"WHAT? THEY DON'T EAT NO MEAT?!"

Take away the above things and what have we got left to eat? Wherever you go, the main topic of conversation for 40 days is, 'What shall we eat?' 'What are you cooking tonight?'

The Fruit and Vegetable stores are doing very well, but the Butcher is suffering.

So after 40 days of eating nothing but Beans and adding to the Global warming problem, it ends. On the 41st. day Cyprus goes mad! The BBQ's come out and every household has a massive binge on MEAT! The day following that is when NOT to go to the Hospital for your medication because it is choca block with people with chronic stomach problems! After 40 days of eating pulses, to eat so much meat suddenly will do this to you!

44.

Law abiding citizens?

Cypriots are great at following rules/laws…NOT! It's almost a defiance every Cypriot is born with. It's a sort of 'You're not telling ME what to do' attitude, not a thought given to the reasons behind said rule or law. For instance…

This is the Police setting us a good example, I mean, what chance have we got?

At the table next to mine…

If roads are for driving on, then pavements MUST be for parking on…right?

We are also very politically correct at all times…while we sleep!

The sign says, 'Girl Wanted' and the bottom right hand corner says, 'Not Blonde'.

What can it mean? What are they insinuating?

???????

Our English isn't great either…

IFIS NOT?

HEE! HEE! HEE!

50.

Well, I have come to the end of another chapter, and unfortunately it's the last in this book. I hope you enjoyed reading it and I hope it made you laugh a few times; it's a great tonic laughter.

I love Cyprus and its people and like I said earlier, once you give in to it and go with THEIR flow, it's amazing here.

END

20124760R00031

Printed in Poland
by Amazon Fulfillment
Poland Sp. z o.o., Wrocław